ADVANCED SW

MASTER THE LANGUAGE'S NUANCES

OLIVER LUCAS JR

Preface

Welcome to the world of Swift, a powerful and expressive programming language that empowers you to create innovative apps for iOS, macOS, watchOS, and tvOS.

This book is your comprehensive guide to mastering Swift, from its fundamental concepts to advanced techniques. Whether you're a seasoned developer or just starting your journey, you'll find valuable insights and practical examples within these pages.

We'll delve into the core language features, such as variables, constants, data types, control flow, and functions. You'll learn how to leverage Swift's type system to write safe and reliable code. We'll explore object-oriented programming concepts, including classes, inheritance, and polymorphism.

Beyond the basics, we'll dive into advanced topics like functional programming, protocol-oriented programming, and concurrency. You'll discover how to write elegant and efficient code using higher-order functions, closures, and asynchronous programming techniques.

To solidify your understanding, we'll provide numerous code examples and exercises throughout the book. You'll have the opportunity to apply what you've learned and build real-world applications.

This book is designed to be your trusted companion as you embark on your Swift programming journey. With dedication and practice, you'll be able to create remarkable apps that delight users.

Happy coding!

TABLE OF CONTENTS

Chapter 5

Chapter 6

Chapter 7

Chapter 8

Chapter 9

Chapter 10

Chapter 1

Deep Dive into Swift's Type System

1.1 Generic Programming in Swift

Generic programming is a powerful technique that allows you to write code that can work with a variety of data types, without sacrificing type safety. In Swift, generics are defined using angle brackets < . . . > and a placeholder type, often represented by T.

Basic Generic Functions

Let's start with a simple example: a generic function to swap two values:

```Swift
func swapTwoValues<T>(_ a: inout T, _ b: inout T) {
    let temporaryA = a
    a = b
    b = temporaryA
}
```

Here, T is a placeholder type. When you call this function, you can pass any two variables of the same type:

```Swift
var x = 10
var y = 20

swapTwoValues(&x, &y)
print(x, y) // Output: 20 10
```

Generic Types

You can also define generic types:

```Swift
struct Stack<Element> {
    var items = [Element]()

    mutating func push(_ item: Element) {
        items.append(item)
    }

    mutating func pop() -> Element? {
        return items.popLast()
    }
}
```

This `Stack` struct can store elements of any type. You can create stacks of integers, strings, or any other custom type.

Advanced Generic Techniques

Generic Constraints:

You can constrain generic types to conform to specific protocols:

```Swift
func findIndex<T: Equatable>(of element: T, in array: [T]) -> Int? {
    for (index, value) in array.enumerated() {
        if value == element {
            return index
        }
    }
    return nil
}
```

Here, T is constrained to be Equatable, meaning it must implement the == operator.

Associated Types:

Associated types allow you to define placeholder types within a protocol:

```swift
Swift
protocol Container {
    associatedtype Item
    var isEmpty: Bool { get }
    mutating func append(_ item: Item)
    var count: Int { get }
}
```

This Container protocol defines an associated type Item, which can be any type.

Generic Subscripts:

You can define generic subscripts to access elements of a collection using a generic index:

```swift
Swift
struct GenericArray<Element> {
    var storage: [Element]

    subscript(index: Int) -> Element {
        get {
            return storage[index]
        }
        set {
            storage[index] = newValue
        }
```

```
    }
}
```

Generic Extensions:

You can extend generic types to add new functionality:

```Swift
extension Array where Element: Equatable {
    func contains(_ element: Element) -> Bool {
        for item in self {
            if item == element {
                return true
            }
        }
        return false
    }
}
```

By understanding and effectively using generic programming, you can write more flexible, reusable, and type-safe Swift code.

1.2 Type Inference and Type Checking in Swift

Type Inference

Swift is a statically typed language, meaning that the type of every variable and expression is known at compile time. However, Swift's powerful type inference system often allows you to omit explicit type annotations, making your code more concise and readable.

The compiler infers types based on the context of the code. For example:

Swift

```swift
let message = "Hello, world!" // Inferred to be of type String
let number = 42 // Inferred to be of type Int
```

Type Checking

Type checking ensures that operations are performed on compatible types. Swift's type checker verifies the correctness of your code at compile time. If it encounters a type mismatch, it will generate an error.

Here are some examples of type checking in action:

Implicit Type Conversion:

Swift performs implicit type conversion in certain cases, such as converting `Int` to `Double` when necessary:

Swift

```swift
let pi = 3.14159
let radius: Double = 5.0
let circumference = 2 * pi * radius // `radius` is implicitly converted to Double
```

Explicit Type Conversion:

In other cases, you may need to explicitly convert types using type casting:

Swift

```swift
let integerValue = 42
let doubleValue = Double(integerValue) // Explicitly convert Int to Double
```

Type Safety:

Swift's strong type system helps prevent many common programming errors. For example, you cannot accidentally assign a string to an integer variable:

Swift
let age: Int = "twenty-five" // This will cause a compile-time error

Generic Types and Type Inference:

Type inference also works with generic types:

```Swift
func swapTwoValues<T>(_ a: inout T, _ b: inout T) {
    let temporaryA = a
    a = b
    b = temporaryA
}

var x = 10
var y = 20
swapTwoValues(&x, &y) // The compiler infers the type of T to be Int
```

By understanding type inference and type checking, you can write more concise, readable, and error-free Swift code.

1.3 Metatypes and Protocol Extensions

Metatypes

A metatype is a type that represents another type. In Swift, you can access the metatype of a type using the `type(of:)` function or the `Type` property.

Why use metatypes?

Type introspection: You can inspect the type of a value at runtime.

Dynamic type checking: You can check the type of a value at runtime and perform conditional actions.

Metaprogramming: You can write generic code that operates on types themselves.

Example:

```Swift
let aString = "Hello, world!"
let stringMetatype = type(of: aString) // Metatype of String

print(stringMetatype) // Output: String.Type
```

Protocol Extensions

Protocol extensions allow you to add functionality to protocols. This is a powerful technique for defining default implementations of methods and properties for conforming types.

Why use protocol extensions?

Code reusability: You can define common functionality for multiple types that conform to a protocol.

Protocol-oriented programming: You can design your code around protocols and their extensions.

Example:

```swift
Swift
protocol Printable {
    func printDescription()
}

extension Printable {
    func printDescription() {
        print("Default implementation")
    }
}

struct Person: Printable {
    var name: String

    func printDescription() {
        print("Name: \(name)")
    }
}

let person = Person(name: "Alice")
person.printDescription() // Output: Name: Alice
```

In this example, the `Printable` protocol defines a `printDescription()` method. The protocol extension provides a default implementation for this method. The `Person` struct conforms to the `Printable` protocol and overrides the default implementation.

Key Points:

Metatypes provide a way to work with types as values at runtime.

Protocol extensions allow you to add functionality to protocols, making your code more flexible and reusable.

By combining metatypes and protocol extensions, you can create powerful and expressive Swift code.

Chapter 2

Functional Programming with Swift

2.1 Higher-Order Functions and Closures

Higher-Order Functions

A higher-order function is a function that takes one or more functions as arguments or returns a function.[1] This concept is fundamental to functional programming and allows for more expressive and concise code.

Example:

```swift
Swift
func applyFunction<T>(function: (T) -> T, to value: T) -> T {
    return function(value)
}

func square(x: Int) -> Int {
    return x * x
}

let result = applyFunction(function: square, to: 5)
print(result) // Output: 25
```

In this example, `applyFunction` is a higher-order function that takes a function `function` as an argument. The `square`function is passed to `applyFunction` and applied to the value `5`.

Closures

A closure is a self-contained block of code that can capture variables from its surrounding context. Closures are a powerful tool for working with higher-order functions and asynchronous programming.

Syntax:

```Swift
{ (parameters) -> return type in
    // code
}
```

Example:

```Swift
let increment = { (x: Int) -> Int in
    return x + 1
}

let result = increment(10)
print(result) // Output: 11
```

Capturing Values:

Closures can capture variables from their enclosing scope:

```Swift
func makeIncrementer(incrementAmount: Int) -> () -> Int {
    var runningTotal = 0

    func increment() -> Int {
        runningTotal += incrementAmount
        return runningTotal
```

```
    }

    return increment
}

let incrementByTen = makeIncrementer(incrementAmount: 10)
print(incrementByTen()) // Output: 10
print(incrementByTen()) // Output: 20
```

Trailing Closures:

If a closure is the last argument to a function, it can be written outside the parentheses:

Swift
```
numbers.sorted { $0 > $1 }
```

Short Form Closures:

If a closure's body is a single expression, you can omit the `return` keyword and the braces:

Swift
```
let sortedNumbers = numbers.sorted { $0 > $1 }
```

Higher-order functions and closures are essential tools for writing expressive and functional Swift code. By mastering these concepts, you can write more concise, elegant, and efficient code.

2.2 Functional Programming Patterns in Swift

Functional programming is a paradigm that emphasizes the use of pure functions, immutability, and higher-order functions. By applying these principles, you can write more concise, readable, and maintainable code.

Here are some common functional programming patterns in Swift:

1. Map, Reduce, and Filter

Map: Applies a function to each element of a collection, returning a new collection with the transformed elements.

Swift
```
let numbers = [1, 2, 3, 4, 5]
let doubledNumbers = numbers.map { $0 * 2 }
```

Reduce: Combines elements of a collection into a single value using a specified combining function.

Swift

```
let sum = numbers.reduce(0) { $0 + $1 }
```

Filter: Creates a new collection containing only the elements that satisfy a given predicate.

Swift

```
let evenNumbers = numbers.filter { $0 % 2 == 0 }
```

2. FlatMap and CompactMap

FlatMap: Maps each element of a sequence to a sequence of values, then flattens the resulting sequences into a single sequence.

Swift

```swift
let nestedArrays = [[1, 2], [3, 4], [5]]
let flattenedArray = nestedArrays.flatMap { $0 }
```

CompactMap: Maps each element of a sequence to an optional value, then removes nil values from the resulting sequence.

Swift

```swift
let strings = ["1", "two", "3", "four"]
let integers = strings.compactMap { Int($0) }
```

3. Recursion

Recursion is a technique where a function calls itself directly or indirectly. It's often used to solve problems that can be broken down[1] into smaller, self-similar subproblems.

Swift

```swift
func factorial(_ n: Int) -> Int {
   if n == 0 {
      return 1
   } else {
      return n * factorial(n - 1)
   }
}
```

4. Higher-Order Functions and Closures

Higher-order functions and closures are fundamental to functional programming. They allow you to create flexible and reusable code.

Swift

```swift
func apply<T>(function: (T) -> T, to value: T) -> T {
```

```
    return function(value)
}
```

```
let doubledValue = apply(function: { $0 * 2 }, to: 5)
```

By understanding and applying these functional programming patterns, you can write more elegant, concise, and maintainable Swift code.

2.3 Result and Optional Chaining

Error Handling with Result

The `Result` enum is a powerful tool for handling errors in a functional and type-safe way. It represents either a success value or a failure, encapsulating the outcome of an operation.

Swift
```
enum Result<Success, Failure> {
    case success(Success)
    case failure(Failure)
}
```

Example:

Swift
```
func divide(x: Int, by y: Int) -> Result<Int, String> {
    guard y != 0 else {
        return .failure("Division by zero")
    }
    return .success(x / y)
}
```

```
let result = divide(x: 10, by: 2)
```

```swift
switch result {
case .success(let quotient):
    print("Result: \(quotient)")
case .failure(let error):
    print("Error: \(error)")
}
```

Chaining Optionals Safely

Optional chaining allows you to access properties and methods of an optional value conditionally. If the optional value is nil, the expression returns nil.

Swift
```swift
let person: Person? = ...
let address = person?.address?.street
```

Optional Binding and Nil-Coalescing Operator

Optional Binding:

Optional binding allows you to safely unwrap an optional value and assign it to a constant or variable.

Swift
```swift
if let unwrappedValue = optionalValue {
    // Use unwrappedValue
}
```

Nil-Coalescing Operator:

The nil-coalescing operator (??) provides a default value if an optional value is nil.

Swift
```
let name = optionalName ?? "Unknown"
```

By combining these techniques, you can write more robust and error-resilient Swift code.

Chapter 3

Concurrency and Asynchronous Programming

3.1 Grand Central Dispatch (GCD)

Grand Central Dispatch (GCD) is a powerful concurrency framework provided by Apple to manage asynchronous tasks efficiently. It allows you to execute tasks concurrently without explicitly managing threads.

Queues

GCD uses queues to organize and execute tasks. There are two main types of queues:

Serial Queues: Tasks are executed one at a time, in the order they are added to the queue.

Concurrent Queues: Multiple tasks can execute concurrently, but the order of execution is not guaranteed.

Creating a Dispatch Queue:

```Swift
let serialQueue = DispatchQueue(label: "com.example.serialQueue")
let concurrentQueue = DispatchQueue(label: "com.example.concurrentQueue", attributes: .concurrent)
```

Adding Tasks to a Queue:

```swift
Swift
serialQueue.async {
    // Task to be executed on the serial queue
}

concurrentQueue.async {
    // Task to be executed on the concurrent queue
}
```

Dispatch Groups

Dispatch groups allow you to synchronize multiple tasks and wait for them to complete.

```swift
Swift
let group = DispatchGroup()

group.enter()
DispatchQueue.global().async {
    // Task 1
    group.leave()
}

group.enter()
DispatchQueue.global().async {
    // Task 2
    group.leave()
}

group.wait() // Wait for both tasks to complete
```

Semaphores and Barriers

Semaphores and barriers are used to control access to shared resources and coordinate task execution.

Semaphores:

A semaphore is a signaling mechanism that allows a specified number of tasks to proceed concurrently.

```swift
Swift
let semaphore = DispatchSemaphore(value: 2) // Allow 2 concurrent tasks

for i in 0..<5 {
    semaphore.wait()
    DispatchQueue.global().async {
        // Critical section
        print("Task \(i) is executing")
        semaphore.signal()
    }
}
```

Barriers:

A barrier block is a special type of task that is guaranteed to execute after all previously submitted tasks have completed.

```swift
Swift
DispatchQueue.global().async {
    // Task 1
}

DispatchQueue.global().async {
    // Task 2
}
```

```swift
DispatchQueue.global().async(flags: .barrier) {
    // Barrier block: Executes after Task 1 and Task 2
    print("All previous tasks have completed")
}
```

By effectively using GCD, you can write highly concurrent and responsive applications in Swift.

3.2 Async/Await: A Modern Approach to Asynchronous Programming

Async/await is a powerful feature in Swift that simplifies asynchronous programming by making it look more like synchronous code. It allows you to write asynchronous code in a sequential style, making it easier to read and reason about.

Asynchronous Functions and Tasks

An asynchronous function is declared with the async keyword and returns an Async<Value> type. This type represents a future value that may not be available immediately.

```swift
Swift
async func fetchData() async -> String {
    // Simulate asynchronous operation
    try await Task.sleep(nanoseconds: 1_000_000_000)
    return "Data fetched successfully"
}
```

To call an asynchronous function, you use the await keyword:

```swift
Swift
let data = await fetchData()
```

```
print(data)
```

Task Groups and Cancellation

Task groups allow you to manage multiple asynchronous tasks concurrently and cancel them if needed.

```
Swift
let group = TaskGroup<String>()

group.addTask {
    try await Task.sleep(nanoseconds: 2_000_000_000)
    return "Task 1"
}

group.addTask {
    try await Task.sleep(nanoseconds: 1_000_000_000)
    return "Task 2"
}

for try await result in group {
    print(result)
}
```

To cancel a task, you can use the `Task.cancel()` method.

Asynchronous Sequences and Streams

Asynchronous sequences and streams provide a way to work with sequences of values that are produced asynchronously.

```
Swift
async func generateNumbers() async -> AsyncStream<Int> {
    for i in 1...10 {
        await Task.sleep(nanoseconds: 500_000_000)
```

```
        yield i
    }
}

for await number in await generateNumbers() {
    print(number)
}
```

Async/await provides a more intuitive and efficient way to write asynchronous code in Swift. By understanding its core concepts, you can create more responsive and scalable applications.

Chapter 4

Memory Management and Performance Optimization

4.1 Reference Counting and ARC

Reference Counting

Reference counting is a memory management technique where objects are kept alive as long as there are references to them. When the reference count of an object reaches zero, it's deallocated.

Automatic Reference Counting (ARC)

ARC is a memory management system that automatically handles reference counting for you. It keeps track of how many references point to an object and deallocates the object when the reference count reaches zero.

Strong, Weak, and Unowned References

Strong References:

The default type of reference.

Increases the reference count of an object.

If a strong reference cycle occurs, it can lead to memory leaks.

Weak References:

Does not increase the reference count of an object.

Can become nil if the object is deallocated.

Often used to break strong reference cycles.

Unowned References:

Similar to weak references, but they don't become nil.

Should only be used when you're certain that the object won't be deallocated before the unowned reference is used.

Can lead to crashes if used incorrectly.

Strong Reference Cycles and How to Break Them

A strong reference cycle occurs when two or more objects have strong references to each other, preventing them from being deallocated.

Breaking Strong Reference Cycles:

Weak References: Use weak references to break the cycle.

Unowned References: Use unowned references when you're certain that the object won't be deallocated before the reference is used.

Weak Self: Use `weak self` or `unowned self` inside closures to avoid strong reference cycles.

```Swift
class Person {
    weak var pet: Pet?
```

```
}

class Pet {
    weak var owner: Person?
}
```

Automatic Reference Counting Performance Implications

While ARC is generally efficient, excessive reference counting can impact performance, especially in large and complex applications. To optimize performance, consider the following:

Minimize Strong Reference Cycles: Use weak and unowned references judiciously to avoid unnecessary retain cycles.

Avoid Unnecessary Retain Cycles: Be mindful of how objects are referenced in closures and delegate patterns.

Profile Your App: Use Instruments to identify potential performance bottlenecks related to memory management.

By understanding these concepts and best practices, you can write efficient and memory-safe Swift code.

4.2 Memory Layout and Optimization Techniques

Struct vs. Class Performance

Structs:

Value types: Copied by value.

Faster to copy and initialize.

More efficient for small, immutable data structures.

Stored on the stack or heap.

Classes:

Reference types: Referenced by pointer.

Slower to copy and initialize.

More flexible for complex data structures with inheritance and polymorphism.

Always stored on the heap.

When to Use Structs:

Small data structures (e.g., points, rectangles, colors)

Immutable data

Data that needs to be copied frequently

When to Use Classes:

Large data structures

Mutable data

Inheritance and polymorphism

Identity-based comparisons

Value Semantics and Copy-on-Write

Value semantics means that when a value type is assigned or passed to a function, a copy of the value is created. This ensures that modifications to the copy do not affect the original value.

Copy-on-Write:

To optimize performance, Swift uses a technique called copy-on-write. This means that when a value type is copied, the system creates a shared reference to the original data. Only when the copy is modified is a new copy created. This can significantly improve performance, especially for large data structures.

Memory Layout and Alignment

The way data is laid out in memory can impact performance. Swift uses memory alignment to optimize memory access. Alignment ensures that data is stored at memory addresses that are multiples of its size. This allows the CPU to access data more efficiently.

Struct Layout:

Fields are laid out sequentially in memory.

Padding may be added to ensure alignment.

Class Layout:

More complex due to reference counting and inheritance.

Includes a reference count, a v-table pointer, and the instance variables.

Alignment is important to optimize memory access.

Optimization Tips:

Use structs for small, immutable data structures.

Use classes for large, mutable data structures.

Be mindful of reference cycles and use weak and unowned references appropriately.

Use copy-on-write to optimize performance.

Consider memory layout and alignment when designing data structuresProfile your app to identify performance bottlenecks.

By understanding these concepts, you can write more efficient and performant Swift code.

4.3 Performance Profiling and Tuning

Using Instruments to Profile Your App

Instruments is a powerful profiling tool included in Xcode. It allows you to analyze your app's performance in real-time or by recording a trace.

Key Instruments for Performance Profiling:

Time Profiler: Identifies time-consuming functions and code blocks.

Allocations Instrument: Tracks memory allocations and deallocations.

Core Animation Instrument: Analyzes rendering performance and frame rate.

Energy Impact Instrument: Measures the energy impact of your app.

Steps to Use Instruments:

Open Instruments: Launch Instruments from Xcode.

Select a Template: Choose a template that suits your needs (e.g., Time Profiler, Allocations).

Profile Your App: Run your app in the Instruments app or attach it to a running app.

Analyze the Results: Identify performance bottlenecks and optimize your code accordingly.

Identifying Bottlenecks and Optimizing Code

Common Performance Bottlenecks:

Inefficient Algorithms: Use algorithms with lower time complexity.

Excessive Object Creation and Destruction: Minimize object creation and use object pooling

Unnecessary Calculations: Optimize calculations and avoid redundant operations.

I/O Operations: Minimize disk and network I/O.

Memory Leaks: Fix memory leaks to prevent memory pressure.

Optimization Techniques:

Use `let` for Immutable Values: Avoid unnecessary copies.

Minimize String Concatenation: Use `String` interpolation or `StringBuilder`

Optimize Loops: Use `for-in` loops for iterating over collections

Use Lazy Properties and Lazy Initialization: Delay initialization until needed.

Profile Your Code: Use Instruments to identify specific performance bottlenecks.

Consider Asynchronous Programming: Use GCD or async/await for long-running tasks.

Understanding Compiler Optimizations

The Swift compiler performs various optimizations to improve code performance. Some of the key optimizations include:

Constant Folding: Evaluating constant expressions at compile time.

Dead Code Elimination: Removing unused code

Loop Optimization: Optimizing loops, such as loop unrolling and strength reduction.

Function Inlining: Inlining small functions to reduce function call overhead.

Tips for Compiler Optimization:

Use `let` for Immutable Values: This allows the compiler to perform more optimizations.

Avoid Unnecessary Complex Expressions: Keep expressions simple and readable.

Use Generic Functions and Types: Generic code can be more efficient.

Consider Using `@inlinable` Attribute: Mark functions as inlinable to encourage the compiler to inline them.

By understanding performance profiling techniques and optimization strategies, you can create high-performance Swift applications that deliver a smooth and responsive user experience.

Chapter 5

Protocol-Oriented Programming

5.1 Protocol Extensions and Default Implementations

Extending Protocols with Default Implementations

Protocol extensions allow you to add default implementations to protocol methods and properties. This can significantly reduce code duplication and improve code maintainability.

Example:

```
Swift
protocol Drawable {
   func draw()
}

extension Drawable {
   func draw() {
      print("Default drawing implementation")
   }
}

struct Circle: Drawable {
   // No need to implement `draw()` here
}

let circle = Circle()
circle.draw() // Output: Default drawing implementation
```

In this example, the `Drawable` protocol declares a `draw()` method. The protocol extension provides a default implementation for this method. The `Circle` struct conforms to the `Drawable` protocol without explicitly implementing the `draw()` method, relying on the default implementation.

Conditional Conformance and Associated Types

Conditional Conformance:

You can constrain protocol extensions to specific types or protocols. This allows you to provide specialized implementations for certain types.

```Swift
protocol Hashable {
    func hash(into hasher: inout Hasher)
}

extension Array: Hashable where Element: Hashable {
    func hash(into hasher: inout Hasher) {
        for element in self {
            hasher.combine(element)
        }
    }
}
```

In this example, the `Array` type conforms to the `Hashable` protocol conditionally, as long as its `Element` type also conforms to `Hashable`.

Associated Types:

Associated types allow you to define placeholder types within a protocol. This enables you to create more flexible and generic protocols.

Swift
```
protocol Container {
    associatedtype Item
    var isEmpty: Bool { get }
    mutating func append(_ item: Item)
    var count: Int { get }
}

struct IntStack: Container {
    typealias Item = Int
    // ...
}
```

In this example, the `Container` protocol defines an associated type `Item`. The `IntStack` struct conforms to the `Container`protocol and specifies that its `Item` type is `Int`.

By effectively using protocol extensions, conditional conformance, and associated types, you can create more flexible, reusable, and type-safe Swift code.

5.2 Protocol Composition

Protocol composition allows you to combine multiple protocols to create more specific requirements for a type. This is a powerful technique for building flexible and modular software architectures.

Combining Multiple Protocols:

To combine multiple protocols, simply list them separated by the & operator:

```Swift
protocol Identifiable & Equatable {
    var id: Int { get }
}
```

A type that conforms to this combined protocol must implement both the `Identifiable` and `Equatable` protocols.

Protocol-Oriented Design Patterns

Protocol-oriented design patterns are a powerful approach to software design in Swift. By using protocols to define behavior and constraints, you can create highly flexible and reusable code.

Common Protocol-Oriented Design Patterns:

Model-View-Controller (MVC):

`Model`: Defines the data model.

`View`: Defines the user interface.

`Controller`: Manages the interaction between the model and the view.

Delegate Pattern:

A protocol defines a set of methods that a delegate object can implement to receive notifications or callbacks from another object.

Observer Pattern:

A protocol defines a set of methods that an observer object can implement to receive notifications from a subject object.

Factory Pattern:

A protocol defines a method for creating objects of a specific type.

Strategy Pattern:

A protocol defines an algorithm or strategy. Different concrete implementations of the protocol can provide different strategies.

Example: A Simple MVC Pattern Using Protocols

```swift
Swift
protocol Model {
    var data: String { get }
}

protocol View {
    func display(data: String)
}

protocol Controller {
    var model: Model { get }
    var view: View { get }

    func updateView()
}

struct MyModel: Model {
    let data = "Hello, world!"
}

struct MyView: View {
```

```swift
    func display(data: String) {
        print(data)
    }
}

struct MyController: Controller {
    let model: MyModel
    let view: MyView

    func updateView() {
        view.display(data: model.data)
    }
}

let controller = MyController(model: MyModel(), view: MyView())
controller.updateView() // Output: Hello, world!
```

By using protocol-oriented design, you can create highly modular, reusable, and testable code.

5.3 Protocol-Oriented Error Handling

Protocol-oriented error handling allows you to define custom error types and error propagation mechanisms using protocols. This approach promotes code reusability and type safety.

Error Handling with Protocols

Defining an Error Protocol:

Swift
```swift
protocol Error: Swift.Error {
    var message: String { get }
}
```

Creating Custom Error Types:

```swift
Swift
struct NetworkError: Error {
   let message: String

   init(message: String) {
      self.message = message
   }
}
```

Throwing Errors from Functions:

```swift
Swift
func fetchData() throws -> Data {
   // ... network request ...
   if let error = error {
      throw NetworkError(message: error.localizedDescription)
   }
   return data
}
```

Handling Errors with `do-catch`:

```swift
Swift
do {
   let data = try fetchData()
   // Process the data
} catch let error as NetworkError {
   print("Network error: \(error.message)")
} catch {
   print("Unknown error")
}
```

Custom Error Types and Error Propagation

By defining custom error types, you can provide more specific error information and tailor error handling to your application's needs.

Example:

```swift
Swift
enum AuthenticationError: Error {
   case invalidCredentials
   case networkError
}

func authenticate(credentials: Credentials) throws -> User {
   // ... authentication logic ...
   if !isValid(credentials) {
      throw AuthenticationError.invalidCredentials
   }

   // ... network request ...
   if let error = error {
      throw AuthenticationError.networkError
   }

   return user
}
```

Error Propagation:

You can propagate errors up the call stack using the `throws` keyword. This allows you to handle errors at higher levels in your code.

```swift
Swift
func processData(data: Data) throws -> Result {
```

```
    // ... data processing ...
    if let error = error {
        throw error
    }
    return result
}
```

By using protocol-oriented error handling, you can create a robust and flexible error handling system in your Swift applications. You can define custom error types, handle errors gracefully, and propagate errors effectively.

Chapter 6

Advanced Property Wrappers

6.1 Custom Property Wrappers

Property wrappers are a powerful feature in Swift that allow you to encapsulate common property behavior in reusable wrappers. You can create custom property wrappers to add functionality like validation, caching, or logging to your properties.

Creating Custom Property Wrappers

To create a custom property wrapper, you define a struct with a `wrappedValue` property and a `projectedValue` property (optional).

```swift
Swift
@propertyWrapper
struct Caching<Value> {
    private var cachedValue: Value?
    private var cachedKey: String?

    var wrappedValue: Value {
        get {
            if let cachedValue = cachedValue, cachedKey == key {
                return cachedValue
            } else {
                let value = calculateValue()
                cachedValue = value
                cachedKey = key
                return value
            }
        }
    }
```

```swift
    set {
        cachedValue = newValue
        cachedKey = key
    }
}

private let key: String

init(wrappedValue: Value, key: String) {
    self.wrappedValue = wrappedValue
    self.key = key
}

var projectedValue: Caching<Value> { self }
}
```

Property Wrappers with Generic Types

You can use generic types to make your property wrappers more flexible. In the `Caching` example, the `Value` type is generic, allowing you to cache values of any type.

Property Wrappers for Read-Only Properties

You can create property wrappers for read-only properties by omitting the `set` accessor in the `wrappedValue` property.

```swift
Swift
@propertyWrapper
struct ReadOnly<Value> {
    let wrappedValue: Value

    init(wrappedValue: Value) {
        self.wrappedValue = wrappedValue
    }
}
```

```
}
```

Using the Property Wrapper:

```swift
Swift
class MyClass {
    @Caching(key: "myValue")
    var myValue: Int = 0
}
```

When you access `myValue`, the `Caching` property wrapper will check if the value is already cached. If it's not, it will calculate the value and store it for future use.

By creating custom property wrappers, you can write more concise and reusable code, as well as enforce specific behavior for your properties.

6.2 Property Wrappers for Side Effects

Property wrappers can be used to add side effects to property access, such as logging, caching, or validation.

Logging Property Access

```swift
Swift
@propertyWrapper
struct Logging<Value> {
    private var value: Value

    var wrappedValue: Value {
        get {
            print("Getting value: \(value)")
            return value
        }
```

```swift
        set {
            print("Setting value: \(newValue)")
            value = newValue
        }
    }
}
```

Caching Property Values

```swift
Swift
@propertyWrapper
struct Cached<Value> {
    private var cachedValue: Value?

    var wrappedValue: Value {
        get {
            if let cachedValue = cachedValue {
                return cachedValue
            } else {
                let value = calculateValue()
                cachedValue = value
                return value
            }
        }
        set {
            cachedValue = newValue
        }
    }

    private func calculateValue() -> Value {
        // Calculate the value
    }
}
```

Validating Property Values

```swift
Swift
@propertyWrapper
struct Validated<Value> {
    private var value: Value?

    var wrappedValue: Value {
        get {
            guard let value = value else {
                fatalError("Value is not set")
            }
            return value
        }
        set {
            guard isValid(newValue) else {
                fatalError("Invalid value")
            }
            value = newValue
        }
    }

    private func isValid(_ value: Value) -> Bool {
        // Validate the value
    }
}
```

Using Property Wrappers for Side Effects

```swift
Swift
class MyClass {
    @Logging
    var name: String = "Alice"

    @Cached
```

```
    var expensiveValue: Int = calculateExpensiveValue()

    @Validated
    var age: Int
}
```

By using property wrappers, you can encapsulate common side effects and make your code more concise and readable.

Chapter 7

Property Observers and KVO

7.1 Property Observers

Property observers allow you to execute code before or after a property's value changes. They are defined using the `willSet` and `didSet` keywords.

`willSet` and `didSet` Observers

`willSet`

Executes before the property's value is set.

Provides access to the new value using the `newValue` keyword.

`didSet`

Executes after the property's value is set.

Provides access to the old value using the `oldValue` keyword.

Example:

```Swift
class Person {
   var name: String {
      willSet {
         print("Name will be changed to \(newValue)")
      }
      didSet {
         print("Name was changed from \(oldValue) to \(name)")
      }
```

```
    }
}
```

Using Property Observers for Side Effects

Property observers can be used to perform various side effects, such as:

Logging: Log changes to the property's value.

Validation: Validate the new value before it's assigned.

Updating Other Properties: Update related properties based on the change.

Triggering Actions: Perform actions, such as sending notifications or updating the UI.

Example: Logging and Validation

```swift
Swift
class Account {
    var balance: Double {
        willSet {
            if newValue < 0 {
                print("Error: Balance cannot be negative")
            }
        }
        didSet {
            print("Balance changed from \(oldValue) to \(balance)")
        }
    }
}
```

Example: Updating Related Properties

```swift
Swift
class Product {
   var price: Double {
      didSet {
         calculateTotalPrice()
      }
   }

   var quantity: Int {
      didSet {
         calculateTotalPrice()
      }
   }

   private var totalPrice: Double = 0

   private func calculateTotalPrice() {
      totalPrice = price * Double(quantity)
   }
}
```

By effectively using property observers, you can create more reactive and dynamic applications. However, it's important to use them judiciously to avoid excessive side effects and potential performance impacts.

7.2 Key-Value Observing (KVO)

Key-Value Observing (KVO) is a mechanism in Cocoa that allows objects to be notified of changes to properties of other objects. This is particularly useful for building reactive and data-driven applications.

Observing Property Changes

To observe a property change, you need to:

Add an Observer:

Use

the `addObserver(_:forKeyPath:options:context:)` method on the observed object.

Specify the observer object, the key path of the property to observe, and the options for the observation.

Implement the `observeValue(forKeyPath:of:change:context:)` **Method:**

This method will be called whenever the observed property changes.

You can access the old and new values of the property, as well as other information about the change.

Example:

```swift
Swift
class Person: NSObject {
    @objc dynamic var name: String = "Alice"
}

class Observer: NSObject {
    func observePerson(person: Person) {
        person.addObserver(self, forKeyPath: #keyPath(Person.name), options: [.new, .old], context: nil)
    }
```

```
    override func observeValue(forKeyPath keyPath: String?, of
object: Any?, change: [NSKeyValueChangeKey : Any]?, context:
UnsafeMutableRawPointer?) {
        if keyPath == #keyPath(Person.name) {
            let newValue = change![NSKeyValueChangeKey.newKey]
as! String
            print("Name changed to \(newValue)")
        }
    }
}
```

KVO Compliance and Best Practices

Dynamic Properties: Use the `@objc dynamic` attribute to make properties KVO-compliant.

Thread Safety: Ensure that KVO notifications are sent from the main thread.

Memory   Management: Use `removeObserver(_:forKeyPath:)` to remove observers when they are no longer needed.

Efficient Observation: Avoid unnecessary observations to improve performance.

KVO and the Observer Pattern

KVO is closely related to the observer pattern, which is a design pattern where objects (observers) are notified of changes in the state of other objects (subjects). KVO provides a convenient way to implement the observer pattern in Cocoa.

Key Differences:

KVO is Built-in: KVO is a built-in mechanism in Cocoa.

Dynamic Properties: KVO requires dynamic properties.

Observer Notification: KVO automatically sends notifications to observers.

Performance Considerations: KVO can be less efficient than custom observer implementations in some cases.

By understanding the principles of KVO and best practices, you can effectively use it to build responsive and data-driven applications.

Chapter 8

Advanced UIKit and SwiftUI

8.1 UIKit Deep Dive

Custom Views and View Controllers

Custom Views:

Subclassing Existing Views: Inherit from existing UIKit views like `UIView`, `UIButton`, or `UILabel` to customize their appearance and behavior.

Creating Custom Views from Scratch: Use `UIView` as the base class to create custom views with custom drawing logic and layout.

Auto Layout: Use Auto Layout to define the layout constraints for your custom views, ensuring they adapt to different screen sizes and orientations.

Drawing with Core Graphics: Use Core Graphics to draw custom shapes, lines, and text directly onto a view's canvas.

Custom View Controllers:

Subclassing Existing View Controllers: Inherit from standard view controllers like `UIViewController`, `UITableViewController`, or `UICollectionViewController` to customize their behavior and UI.

Creating Custom View Controllers from Scratch: Use `UIViewController` as the base class to create custom view controllers with custom view hierarchies and logic.

Segue-Based Navigation: Use segues to transition between view controllers.

Programmatic Navigation: Use `UINavigationController` and `UIPresentationController` to programmatically manage navigation and presentation of view controllers.

Core Animation and Custom Transitions

Core Animation is a powerful framework for creating animations and visual effects in UIKit apps.

Key Concepts:

Layers: Layers are the building blocks of Core Animation. Each view has a backing layer that can be manipulated to create animations.

CALayer: The base class for all layers.

CAAnimation: The base class for all animations.

CATransaction: A transaction is a group of animations that can be committed together.

Custom Transitions:

Customizing Standard Transitions: Use `UIViewControllerAnimatedTransitioning` to customize the appearance and behavior of standard transitions like push, pop, present, and dismiss.

Creating Custom Transitions: Use `UIViewControllerAnimatedTransitioning` to create entirely custom transitions, such as interactive transitions or complex animations.

UIKit Performance Optimization

Key Techniques:

Cell Reuse: Reuse table view cells and collection view cells to improve scrolling performance.

Image Optimization: Optimize image size and format, and use image caching.

Asynchronous Tasks: Offload heavy tasks to background threads using GCD or Operation Queues.

Core Animation Performance: Avoid overusing Core Animation and optimize layer hierarchies.

Auto Layout Performance: Be mindful of complex Auto Layout constraints, as they can impact performance.

Profiling: Use Instruments to identify performance bottlenecks and optimize accordingly.

By mastering these techniques, you can create highly customized, performant, and visually appealing UIKit applications.

8.2 SwiftUI in Depth

Advanced SwiftUI Layouts and Data Flow

Advanced Layouts:

GeometryReader: Use `GeometryReader` to dynamically size and position views based on their available space.

ZStack: Layer views on top of each other to create complex layouts.

MatchedGeometryEffect: Create visually appealing transitions between views.

CoordinateSpace: Customize coordinate systems for precise positioning and alignment.

Data Flow:

State: Manage mutable state within a view using the `@State` property wrapper.

Environment: Share global data across multiple views using the `@Environment` property wrapper.

ObservedObject: Observe changes in a complex object and trigger view updates.

StateObject: Create a single source of truth for a view hierarchy.

Custom Views and Modifiers

Custom Views:

Creating Custom Views: Define custom views using `struct` and the `View` protocol.

View Builders: Use view builders to construct complex views declaratively.

Environment Values: Access and modify environment values within custom views.

Custom Modifiers:

Creating Custom Modifiers: Define custom modifiers using function builders.

Chaining Modifiers: Chain multiple modifiers together to create complex effects.

Conditional Modifiers: Use conditional logic to apply modifiers conditionally.

SwiftUI Performance Optimization

Reduce State Updates: Minimize unnecessary state updates to improve performance.

Optimize View Hierarchy: Keep your view hierarchy as simple as possible.

Use Lazy VStacks and Lazy HStacks: Lazy loading can improve performance for large lists.

Optimize Image Loading: Use `AsyncImage` with appropriate caching and resizing.

Profile Your App: Use Xcode's Instruments to identify performance bottlenecks.

By mastering these advanced techniques, you can create complex, performant, and visually appealing SwiftUI applications.

Chapter 9

Testing and Debugging Swift Apps

9.1 Unit Testing with XCTest

XCTest is a powerful testing framework provided by Apple for writing unit tests in Swift. Unit tests help ensure the correctness and reliability of your code.

Writing Effective Unit Tests

Key Principles:

Test a Single Unit of Code: Focus on testing individual functions, methods, or types in isolation.

Keep Tests Independent: Avoid dependencies between tests to ensure they can be run in any order.

Write Clear and Concise Tests: Use descriptive test names and comments to explain the test's purpose.

Test Edge Cases: Consider boundary conditions, invalid input, and error handling.

Test Negative Scenarios: Ensure your code handles errors and unexpected input gracefully.

Basic Structure of a Test Case:

```swift
Swift
import XCTest

class MyTestClassTests: XCTestCase {
    func testExample() {
```

```
    // Arrange
    let input = ...
    let expectedOutput = ...

    // Act
    let actualOutput = myFunction(input)

    // Assert
    XCTAssertEqual(actualOutput, expectedOutput)
  }
}
```

Testing Asynchronous Code

Using XCTestExpectations:

Swift
```
func testAsynchronousOperation() {
    let expectation = XCTestExpectation(description: "Operation
completed")

    asyncOperation {
      // ... asynchronous operation ...
      expectation.fulfill()
    }

    wait(for: [expectation], timeout: 5.0)
}
```

Using XCTestCase.waitForExpectations:

Swift
```
func testAsynchronousOperation() {
```

```
        let expectation = expectation(description: "Operation
completed")

    asyncOperation {
        // ... asynchronous operation ...
        expectation.fulfill()
    }

    waitForExpectations(timeout: 5.0)
}
```

Mocking and Dependency Injection

Mocking:

Mocking involves creating fake objects that simulate the behavior of real objects, allowing you to isolate the unit under test.

Dependency Injection:

Dependency injection is a technique for providing dependencies to a class or function. This makes testing easier by allowing you to inject mock objects.

Example:

```
Swift
class NetworkService {
    func fetchData() -> String {
        // ... network request ...
    }
}

class MyService {
    private let networkService: NetworkService
```

```swift
    init(networkService: NetworkService) {
        self.networkService = networkService
    }

    func processData() -> String {
        let data = networkService.fetchData()
        // ... process data ...
    }
}

// In the test case:
class MyServiceTests: XCTestCase {
    func testProcessData() {
        let mockNetworkService = MockNetworkService()
        mockNetworkService.fetchDataStub = { "Test Data" }

        let myService = MyService(networkService: mockNetworkService)
        let result = myService.processData()

        XCTAssertEqual(result, "Processed Test Data")
    }
}
```

By writing comprehensive unit tests and using techniques like mocking and dependency injection, you can improve the quality, reliability, and maintainability of your Swift code.

9.2 UI Testing with XCTest

UI Testing allows you to automate the interaction with your app's user interface. It's a valuable tool for ensuring the quality and user experience of your app.

Writing UI Tests

To write UI tests, you'll use the XCTestCase class and the XCUIApplication class to interact with your app's UI elements.

Basic Structure of a UI Test:

```swift
Swift
import XCTest

class MyUITests: XCTestCase {
   func testExample() {
      let app = XCUIApplication()
      app.launch()

      // Find and interact with UI elements
      let button = app.buttons["Login"]
      button.tap()

      // Make assertions
      XCTAssertTrue(app.staticTexts["Welcome"].exists)
   }
}
```

Testing User Interactions and Assertions

Common UI Interactions:

Tap: element.tap()

Type Text: element.typeText("Hello")

Swipe: element.swipeLeft(), element.swipeRight(), etc.

Scroll: `element.swipeUp()`, `element.swipeDown()`, etc.

Making Assertions:

Existence: `XCTAssertTrue(element.exists)`

Visibility: `XCTAssertTrue(element.isHittable)`

Text   Content: `XCTAssertEqual(element.label,`
`"Expected Text")`

State: `XCTAssertTrue(element.isSelected)`

Example: Testing a Login Screen

```Swift
func testLogin() {
    let app = XCUIApplication()
    app.launch()

    let usernameField = app.textFields["Username"]
    usernameField.tap()
    usernameField.typeText("testuser")

    let passwordField = app.secureTextFields["Password"]
    passwordField.tap()
    passwordField.typeText("testpassword")

    let loginButton = app.buttons["Login"]
    loginButton.tap()

    XCTAssertTrue(app.staticTexts["Welcome, testuser!"].exists)
}
```

Tips for Effective UI Testing:

Identify Critical User Flows: Focus on testing the most important user journeys.

Keep Tests Maintainable: Use clear and concise test names and comments.

Avoid Flaky Tests: Use appropriate waiting mechanisms and assertions to ensure test reliability.

Use Test Recording: Xcode's test recorder can help you generate UI tests quickly.

Prioritize Test Execution: Run critical tests more frequently.

By writing comprehensive UI tests, you can improve the quality and user experience of your app.

9.3 Debugging Techniques

Using the LLDB Debugger

LLDB is a powerful debugger that can be used to inspect your code's execution at runtime. Here are some key techniques to use with LLDB:

Breakpoints: Set breakpoints to pause execution at specific lines of code.

Step Over: Execute the current line of code and move to the next one.

Step Into: Step into a function call to examine its execution.

Step Out: Step out of the current function and return to the caller.

Print Variables: Use the `print` command to inspect the values of variables.

Examine Memory: Use the `memory read` command to examine memory contents.

Breakpoints and Stepping Through Code

Breakpoints allow you to pause execution at a specific point in your code. You can set breakpoints in the Xcode source editor or using LLDB commands.

Once you've set a breakpoint, you can use the step commands to control the execution of your code:

Step Over: Executes the current line of code and moves to the next one.

Step Into: Steps into a function call, allowing you to examine its execution.

Step Out: Steps out of the current function and returns to the caller.

Debugging Asynchronous Code

Debugging asynchronous code can be more challenging due to its non-linear nature. Here are some techniques to help you debug asynchronous code:

Breakpoints in Asynchronous Functions: Set breakpoints within asynchronous functions to pause execution at specific points.

LLDB Commands for Asynchronous Tasks: Use LLDB commands like `thread list` and `thread return` to inspect and control asynchronous tasks.

Logging: Use `print` statements or a logging framework to log information about the execution of asynchronous code.

Testing: Write unit tests to verify the behavior of asynchronous code.

Profiling: Use Instruments to identify performance bottlenecks and asynchronous issues.

By effectively using these debugging techniques, you can identify and fix bugs more efficiently, leading to higher-quality and more reliable code.

Chapter 10

Advanced Topics in Swift

10.1 Result Builders

Result builders are a powerful feature in Swift that allow you to construct complex data structures and UI layouts in a declarative and concise way. They are particularly useful for building SwiftUI views and other structured data.

Creating Custom Result Builders

To create a custom result builder, you define a function builder attribute and a builder function:

```Swift
@resultBuilder
struct MyBuilder {
    static func buildBlock(_ components: Component...) -> ComponentContainer {
    // Combine components into a container
  }
}
```

The `buildBlock` function takes a variadic parameter of `Component` and returns a `ComponentContainer`. The components can be any type, and the builder function can combine them in any way.

Result Builders for SwiftUI and Other Frameworks

SwiftUI extensively uses result builders to construct views declaratively:

```swift
Swift
struct MyView: View {
    var body: some View {
        VStack {
            Text("Hello, world!")
            Image(systemName: "globe")
        }
    }
}
```

The VStack view builder combines its child views into a vertical stack.

Other frameworks, such as Combine, also use result builders to define pipelines of asynchronous operations:

```swift
Swift
let publisher = Publishers.CombineLatest(
    publisher1,
    publisher2
) { value1, value2 in
    // Combine values
}
```

By understanding and using result builders effectively, you can write more concise and expressive code, especially when building complex UI layouts and data structures.

10.2 Property Delegates

Property delegates provide a way to encapsulate the logic of accessing and setting a property's value. They allow you to add custom behavior to properties, such as caching, validation, or synchronization.

Implementing Custom Property Delegates

To implement a custom property delegate, you define a struct with a `wrappedValue` property and a `projectedValue`property (optional).

```swift
Swift
@propertyDelegate
struct Caching<Value> {
   private var cachedValue: Value?

   var wrappedValue: Value {
      get {
         if let cachedValue = cachedValue {
            return cachedValue
         } else {
            let value = calculateValue()
            cachedValue = value
            return value
         }
      }
      set {
         cachedValue = newValue
      }
   }

   private func calculateValue() -> Value {
      // Calculate the value
   }
}
```

Using Property Delegates for Lazy Initialization and Thread Safety

Lazy Initialization:

```swift
Swift
@propertyDelegate
struct Lazy<Value> {
  private var _value: Value?
  private let initializer: () -> Value

  var wrappedValue: Value {
    mutating get {
      if let value = _value {
        return value
      } else {
        let value = initializer()
        _value = value
        return value
      }
    }
    set {
      _value = newValue
    }
  }

  init(initializer: @escaping () -> Value) {
    self.initializer = initializer
  }
}
```

Thread Safety:

```swift
Swift
@propertyDelegate
struct ThreadSafe<Value> {
   private var _value: Value?
            private   let   queue   =   DispatchQueue(label:
"com.example.threadSafe")

   var wrappedValue: Value {
     get {
       queue.sync { _value! }
     }
     set {
       queue.sync { _value = newValue }
     }
   }
}
```

Example Usage:

```swift
Swift
class MyClass {
   @Lazy var expensiveValue: Int = {
     // Expensive calculation
   }()

   @ThreadSafe var sharedValue: Int = 0
}
```

By using property delegates, you can write more concise and reusable code, as well as enforce specific behavior for your properties.

10.3 Swift Macros

Swift Macros are a powerful language feature that allows you to extend the language itself. They provide a way to generate code at compile time, enabling powerful metaprogramming techniques.

Writing Custom Macros

To define a custom macro, you use the @attached attribute and the macro keyword:

```
Swift
@attached(member)
public macro MyMacro() = #function
```

This macro, when applied to a function, will replace the function's name with the string "MyMacro".

Macro Expansion and Syntax

Macro expansion involves transforming the macro's syntax into actual Swift code. Swift provides a macro expansion syntax that you can use within your macro definitions:

```
Swift
@attached(member)
public macro MyMacro<T>() = #[
   func myMacroFunction<T>(_ value: T) -> T {
     // Macro body
   }
]
```

Here, the # symbol is used to introduce macro syntax elements. The #[...] syntax is used to define a block of code that will be expanded into the final Swift code.

Key Macro Syntax Elements:

#function: Expands to the name of the current function.

#file: Expands to the name of the current file.

#line: Expands to the current line number.

#column: Expands to the current column number.

#expr: Expands to the expression that follows it.

#token: Expands to the next token in the input.

Example: A Simple Macro

```Swift
@attached(member)
public macro Log() = #[
    print(#function)
]
```

You can use this macro to log the name of the current function:

```Swift
func myFunction() {
    @Log
    ()
}
```

This will expand to:

```swift
Swift
func myFunction() {
    print("myFunction")
}
```

By understanding the basics of macro syntax and expansion, you can create powerful and expressive macros to extend the capabilities of the Swift language.